Union Pacific System

A Glimpse of Great Salt Lake, Utah

Union Pacific System

A Glimpse of Great Salt Lake, Utah

ISBN/EAN: 9783337247706

Printed in Europe, USA, Canada, Australia, Japan

Cover: Foto ©Andreas Hilbeck / pixelio.de

More available books at **www.hansebooks.com**

IDAHO

BOX ELDER

Preston
Weston
Franklin
Richmond
Ransom
(Trenton P. O.)
Smithfield
Hyde Park
Cachill
Logan
Cache Jc.
Collinston
Dewey
Mendon
Honeyville
BOX ELDER LAKE
Brigham or
Box Elder C. H.
Craighead
Willard
HOT SPRINGS

HANSEL MTS.
HANSEL SPRING VALLEY
RANGE
WEST MOUNTAINS
Monument
Lake
Rozel
Promontory Spur
Blue Creek
Corinne
Brigham Sta.
Curry

PROMONTORY
PACIFIC

SOUTH'N
Felton
Seco
Ombey
Matlin

TERRACE RANGE

GREAT

DOLPHIN ISLAND
LION CLIFF
CROW'S NEST PEAK
PELICAN BAY
GUNNISON ISLAND
STRONGS KNOB
Dart Straits

AMERICAN
DESERT

SALT

BEAR RIVER BAY

MUD IS.

WEBER
OGDEN
Ogden River
Uintal

FREMONT
ISLAND
Spring
ROSARIO BEACH
Hooper
Syracuse Jc.
WEBER CANON
Layton
Kaysville

SYRACUSE

ANTELOPE
WHITE ROCK
OR
ELEPHANT HEAD
CHURCH
ISLAND
ANTELOPE ISLAND

LAKESIDE
Farmington
Centreville
Island Farm
Woods Cross

HAT OR ROCK I.
CARRINGTON ISLAND

LAKESIDE RANGE

LAKE

STANSBURY ISLAND

SHEEP ROCK
BLACK ROCK
HOT SPRING LAKE
SALT LAKE CITY
Chambers

CEDAR RANGE

ALKALI
FLATS

The Great
SALT LAKE
ON
UNION
PACIFIC

TOOELE

GARFIELD BEACH
S R A W L T
Morgan
Francklyn
Germania
Lovendahl's
Sandy

TUILLA MTS.
Lake Point
Half Way House
Tooele
Terminus
RUSH LAKE
Stockton

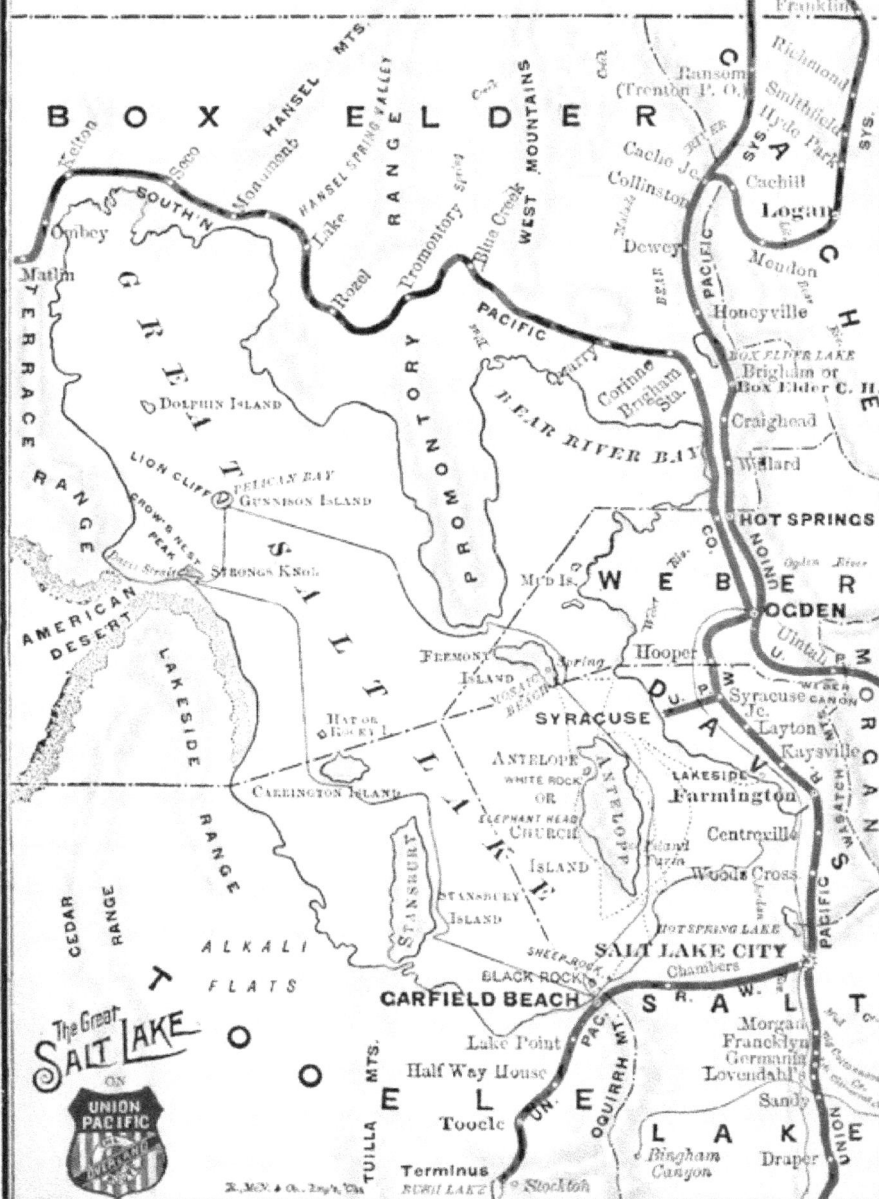

OQUIRRH MT.

L A K E
Bingham Canyon
Draper

UNION PACIFIC

WASATCH

MORGAN

Rand, McNally & Co., Eng'rs, Chic.

Pavilion at Garfield Beach, Great Salt Lake—on the Union Pacific System.

A GLIMPSE

OF

GREAT SALT LAKE

UTAH.

ILLUSTRATED.

ON THE LINE OF

The Union Pacific System,

"THE OVERLAND ROUTE."

1892.

UNION PACIFIC
THE OVERLAND ROUTE

Presented with Compliments   Illustrated from

Passenger Department   ⁂   Original Sketches by

Union Pacific System   Mr. Alfred Lambourne

PRINTERS

LIST OF AGENTS.

Boston, Mass.,—290 Washington Street.
W. S. CONDELL, New England Freight and Passenger Agent.
E. M. NEWBEGIN, Traveling Freight and Passenger Agent.

Butte, Mont.—Corner Main and Broadway.
E. Y. MAZE, General Agent.

Chattanooga, Tenn.—P. O. Box 543.
F. L. LYNDE, Traveling Passenger Agent.

Cheyenne, Wyo.
C. W. SWEET, Ticket and Freight Agent.

Chicago, Ill.,—191 South Clark Street.
W. H. KNIGHT, General Agent Freight and Passenger Departments.
T. W. YOUNG, Traveling Passenger Agent.
D. W. JOHNSTON, Traveling Passenger Agent.
W. T. HOLLY, City Passenger Agent.

Cincinnati, Ohio—27 West Fourth Street.
J. D. WELCH, General Agent Freight and Passenger Departments.
A. G. SHEARMAN, Traveling Freight and Passenger Agent.
T. C. HIRST, Traveling Passenger Agent.

Council Bluffs, Iowa.
A. J. MANDERSON, General Agent, U. P. Transfer.
B. W. CHAMBERLAIN, Passenger Agent.
J. W. MAYNARD, Ticket Agent.
J. C. MITCHELL, City Ticket Agent, 421 Broadway.

Denver, Col.—1703 Larimer Street.
GEO. ADY, General Agent.
C. H. TITUS, Traveling Passenger Agent.
E. G. PATTERSON, City Ticket Agent.
F. G. ERB, City Passenger Agent.
E. F. LACKNER, Ticket Agent, Union Depot.

Des Moines, Iowa—218 Fourth Street.
E. M. FORD, Traveling Passenger Agent.

Ft. Worth, Texas.
D. B. KEELER, General Freight and Passenger Agent Ft. Worth & Denver City Railway.
A. J. RATCLIFFE, General Passenger Agent.
N. S. DAVIS, City Ticket Agent, 301 Main Street.

Helena, Mont.—28 North Main Street.
H. O. WILSON, Freight and Passenger Agent.

Kansas City, Mo.—1038 Union Avenue.
J. B. FRAWLEY, General Agent.
J. B. REESE, Traveling Passenger Agent.
H. K. PROUDFIT, City Passenger Agent.
T. A. SHAW, Ticket Agent
C. A. WHITTIER, City Ticket Agent, 1000 Main Street.
A. W. MILLSPAUGH, Ticket Agent, Union Depot.

London, England—Ludgate Circus.
THOS. COOK & SON, European Passenger Agents.

Los Angeles, Cal.—229 South Spring Street.
G. F. HERR, Passenger Agent.

New Whatcom, Wash.
J. W. ALTON, General Agent.

New York City—287 Broadway.
R. TENBROECK, General Eastern Agent.
J. D. TENBROECK, Traveling Passenger Agent.
S. A. HUTCHISON, Traveling Passenger Agent.
WM. A. DOLAN, Traveling Passenger Agent.
J. F. WILEY, City Passenger Agent.

Oakland, Cal.—Twelfth and Broadway.
GEO. B. SEAMAN, Passenger Agent.

Ogden, Utah—Union Depot.
C. A. HENRY, Ticket Agent.

Olympia, Wash.—Percival's Wharf.
J. C. PERCIVAL, Ticket Agent.

Omaha, Neb.—1302 Farnam Street.
HARRY P. DEUEL, City Ticket Agent.
FRANK N. PROPHET, City Passenger Agent.
M. J. GREEVY, Traveling Passenger Agent, Ninth and Farnam Streets.
J. K. CHAMBERS, Ticket Agent, Union Depot.

Pittsburg, Pa.,—400 Wood Street.
S. C. MILBOURNE, Traveling Passenger Agent.

Portland, Ore.—54 Washington Street.
W. H. HURLBURT, Assistant General Passenger Agent.
GEO. H. HILL, Traveling Passenger Agent.
V. A. SCHILLING, City Ticket Agent.
A. J. GOODRICH, City Passenger Agent.
A. L. MAXWELL, Ticket Agent, Grand Central Station.

Port Angeles, Wash.
R. R. HARDING, Agent.

Port Townsend, Wash.,—Union Wharf.
H. L. TIBBALS, Ticket Agent.

Pueblo, Colo.—233 North Union Avenue.
A. S. CUTHBERTSON, General Agent.

St. Joseph, Mo.—Chamber of Commerce.
S. M. ADSIT, General Freight and Passenger Agent St. Joseph & Grand Island Railroad.
F. P. WADE, City Ticket Agent, corner Third and Francis Streets.
JO. HANSON, Ticket Agent, Union Depot.

St. Louis, Mo.—213 North Fourth Street.
J. F. AGLAR, General Agent Freight and Passenger Departments.
N. HAIGHT, Traveling Passenger Agent.
E. R. TUTTLE, Traveling Passenger Agent.
E. A. WILLIAMS, City Freight and Passenger Agent

Salt Lake City, Utah—201 Main Street.
D. E. BURLEY, General Agent.
C. E. INGALLS, Traveling Passenger Agent.
C. P. CANFIELD, Traveling Passenger Agent.
F. F. ECCLES, City Ticket Agent.
W. S. EVANS, City Passenger Agent.

San Francisco, Cal.—1 Montgomery Street.
D. W. HITCHCOCK, General Agent.
MALONE JOYCE, Traveling Passenger Agent.
W. R. VICE, Pacific Coast Passenger Agent.
J. F. FUGAZI, Emigration Agent, 19 Montgomery Avenue.

Seattle, Wash.—705 Second Street.
A. C. MARTIN, General Agent.

Sioux City, Iowa—303 Fourth Street.
D. M. COLLINS, General Agent.
GEO. E. ABBOTT, Traveling Freight and Passenger Agent.
H. M. BIRDSALL, City Ticket Agent.
GEO. LEDYARD, City Passenger Agent.
GEO. F. WHEELOCK, Ticket Agent, Union Depot.

Spokane, Wash.—Corner Riverside and Washington
PERRY GRIFFIN, Passenger and Ticket Agent.

Tacoma, Wash.—903 Pacific Avenue.
E. E. ELLIS, General Agent.

Trinidad, Colo.
J. F. LINTHURST, Ticket Agent.

Victoria, B. C.—100 Government Street.
C. G. RAWLINGS, General Agent.

E. L. LOMAX,
GENERAL PASSENGER AND TICKET AGENT.

J. N. BROWN,
ACTING ASST. GEN'L PASS'R AND TKT. AGT.,

OMAHA, NEB.

(5)

Black Rock, from the Sand Dunes, Great Salt Lake—reached via the Union Pacific System

A Glimpse of Great Salt Lake.

BEFORE proceeding with a short narration of the sights and incidents of an extended cruise on Utah's Inland Sea, it will, perhaps, be well to first state briefly the purpose which led the writer to take such an exceptional degree of interest in that comparatively unknown body of water, and then, for the better understanding of the descriptive parts, give an outline sketch of the sea itself. I call the body of water a sea, although it is set down on the map of Utah as a lake, not only from the fact that it is often so called, but because its every characteristic makes more suitable the former name. The several cruises which were made, and which formed a complete circuit of the sea, were undertaken partly for pleasure and partly for the purpose of exploration, and the writer accompanied them through a desire to make a set of sketches—the islands and shores, with their attendant phenomena of water and sky. This design had been suggested by a perusal of Captain Stansbury's book, and from watching the phases of storm and sunshine, as seen from the southern mainland and one of the islands already visited. * Stansbury told how much of interest might be seen on a cruise that would comprehend the entire sea; for despite the forbidding nature of its low shores, made ugly by slime and alkali, there are other, less seen portions, either

---

* Captain Stansbury made the first survey of the Great Salt Lake in 1849–50. Stansbury Island was named after him; Gunnison Island after Lieutenant Gunnison in his command. Frémont's visit to the island now bearing his name was in 1843; he called it, at the time, Disappointment Island. The first mention of the lake was made by Baron La Hontan in 1689. A Mr. Miller, of the Jacob Astor party, stood by its shore in 1820, and Mr. John Bedyear in 1825. Members of Captain Bonneville's expedition looked upon the scene from near the mouth of Ogden River in 1833. Bonneville himself gave a rather fanciful description of the lake, as seen from a mountain-side (as told in Irving), though it is not certain if he was ever an eye-witness of the scene himself. His name has been given to a great fossil lake of the Quaternary period, whose shore-line may be now seen throughout the neighboring valleys, and of which the present Great Salt Lake is but the bitter fragment.

Sheep Rock and Points of Oquirrh, Great Salt Lake—reached via the Union Pacific System.

grand or novel, where the clear green water washes on beaches of sand or pebbles, or at the feet of gigantic cliffs. In display of color also, the place is remarkable, the sky and water being strikingly beautiful, tender, vivid, even gorgeous at times, beyond what can be seen elsewhere, save in the tropic zone.

Glancing at the accompanying map, we find that this elevated basin of water, lake, or sea, as we may hereafter choose to call it, is somewhat peculiar in outline, resembling slightly a human hand, the fingers pressed together and pointing north-northwest. The portion of water forming the thumb is known as Bear River Bay, and the dividing mountains, between thumb and fingers, as Promontory Range. In the palm of the hand are four large islands—Antelope, Stansbury, Carrington, and Fremont. Away to the north are three that are smaller—Strong's Knob, Gunnison, and Dolphin. Along the eastern shore are the Wahsatch Mountains; on the south and west, the Oquirrh, the Terrace, and other portions of the Desert Range. Seven streams empty their waters into its briny depths, and yet its saline density remains ever the same. The largest of the streams are the Jordan, the Weber, and the Bear; the two latter entering on the northeast, their source being away to the eastward among the Uintah Mountains. The first enters on the southeast, coming from a large, fresh-water lake, about thirty miles to the south, and which is fed by the torrents pouring down from the Wahsatch. The surface of this strange briny sea has an annual rise and fall of from fifteen to eighteen inches, being highest about the middle of June and lowest toward the end of November. This variation in rise and fall is due to the wetness or dryness of the seasons, as would of course be imagined. The mouths of the various streams form extensive marshes, entering as they all do where the shores are low. They are the haunt of the usual marsh birds: coots, divers, snipe, and wild duck; besides larger birds, as geese, herons, pelicans, and occasionally a wild swan.

It was on June 14 that our yacht was ready to sail. Our party of six was under the guidance of a most efficient captain—one who, in all probability, is more familiar than any other man with the moods of the inland sea. He was also owner of the boat, whose construction he had superintended; and as it has been demonstrated to be an excellent craft to buffet with those heavy waves, some interest may attach to its special build. In dimensions it is twenty-one feet over all, ten feet beam. The hull, or rather hulls, for although the boat is classed as a yacht, it is partly of a catamaran build, are constructed so as to offer the least possible resistance to the dense water, while at the same time keeping her perfectly free from the danger of upsetting. In canvas it carries a main and a jib, a gaff, and a jib-topsail; is managed by a double rudder, and in every detail the peculiar exigencies to be met have been well considered.

At starting it was proposed to keep a log; a record of our cruise, the shifting of winds, the varying of our course, with all the multiplicity of incidents that befall the mariner. But after the first thirty hours the idea was

Twilight at the Marshes, Great Salt Lake—reached via the Union Pacific System.

abandoned. Save for the few jottings from which this account is penned, we let winds and waves go as they list, without a thought beyond the pleasure or immediate duty of the hour. Our course for those first thirty hours was up the eastern shore of Antelope Island, in point of scenery the least attractive of the entire circuit, though during our progress we were treated to a series of striking effects in the forming and breaking of sudden storms. The island on its eastern side has no bold features, its tall, dark hills sloping down to the water's edge in commonplace, rounded forms, or with broad, flat, sage-covered spaces between their feet and the shore. Commencing with our departure from Garfield Beach, the noted resort on the southern shore, I will condense that part of our cruise into a couple of paragraphs:

"Cast off from the pier at Garfield, hoisted sail, and bore in the direction of Black Rock. Lake quiet, weather sultry. Along the eastern horizon yellow-headed cumuli; overhead, ragged drift. To windward, southwest, a portentous heap of cloud, riven, at times, by lightning. Touched at the sand dunes near Saltair, and then steered our course for Antelope Island. At twilight a sudden squall from the south, coming down from the Oquirrh summits, and throwing up waves choppy and disagreeable. Sky cleared of clouds at 10 p. m., giving a splendid moonlight run to Island Farm, on the eastern shore of Antelope.

"Sunrise of the next day, calm and bright. Sails set at 9 a. m. to make but slow progress, with winds light and variable, alternated with dead calms. Lake very blue all day, with soft, white clouds peeping up all day around the horizon. Off Ragged Point at 6 p. m., and soon after a strange phenomenon observed. From distant headlands to westward came floating a magic fleet. It looked as if the bowlders of the shore had started out lakeward, or more properly, as if they had been changed into huge white snowballs, and then sent rolling onward across the waters. As they approached more near, we found them to be great globes of foam, formed by the beating of briny waves among the rocks, and then cast adrift by a shifting wind. At sunset a strong gale commenced to blow, issuing from the north-northwest, and increasing each moment in force and power. Unable to beat against it, we cast anchor in the nearest bay, one sheltered somewhat on the west, but unfortunately open to the north. At twilight a wild and thrilling spectacle. The wind had grown stronger, the waves higher. In almost ocean size they came hurrying from windward, tossing their white manes, sweeping past us in thick-set ranks, to burst on the shore in a deluge of foam. Straining at its cable, our yacht staggered with each blow of the heavy water; while from mast and rigging came an answering whistle to the blast. Across the lake, to the north and northwest, a strange crystalline light illumined the air. To the west, a lurid glare of color streamed upward on the wind-torn clouds, finding an echo on the far-off Weber Cliffs. To the east, the sky was all but cloudless; the lake a cold, sheeny green; and across its

Wahsatch Mountains, from Fremont Island, Great Salt Lake—reached via the Union Pacific System.

whirling surface lay a shivering trail of pallid gray, pointing where the moon, dim and pale, the ghost of a dead world, lifted above the distant Wahsatch peaks, and stared at the acrid waters of a dead sea. At 11 p. m. the winds abating, the waves sinking, the sky clearing. All quiet on board our yacht."

A beautiful sight accompanied the following dawn. It was Venus as morning star, making the east lovely with her clear white light. Not a speck or thread of cloud was in the sky from which she smiled upon us. So glassy calm lay the waters, it seemed scarcely possible they had raged so fiercely the night before; and so clear they were, we could see the bowlders on the lake-bed full thirty feet below.

Breakfast over, and our anchor raised, we made an unpleasant discovery. The strain imposed upon it had broken the ring; one of the rudders, also, had been torn from its lower fastening; so these discoveries, combined with the fact that we had neglected to bring extra fittings, made a retrograde movement necessary. We managed to run across to the nearest point on the eastern shore, and one of our party was detailed to seek the necessary articles at the nearest village. As this was some distance away, we lay at rest, waiting his return, until the middle of the afternoon.

The dreariness of the shore, where we lay at anchor, was oppressive to see. It was a low, clay bank, of a grayish red, and dotted with grease-wood bushes of stunted growth. Very little life disturbed its solitude. Two or three querulous snipe ran along the margin; a couple of brown divers sported on the near water; and once or twice a string of broad-winged pelicans sailed overhead. In the brooding mid-day calms, such pieces of the low shore become repellent; nor does the limitless scope of horizon serve to dispel the feeling of dejection they inspire. The mind is then as much weighed down by the sense of infinity in the distant mountain chains as by the sterility of the nearer shore. There in our sight stretched out a hundred and fifty miles of the Wahsatch Range; Oquirrh, with their endless recurrence of peak and gorge—the sixteen miles of Antelope occupying but a fragment on the western horizon; the precipitous sides of Stansbury, with vista after vista of the Desert Range, leading the eye around to Fremont and Promontory; and these latter, lengthening out by peak and slope, and peak again, directing the sight to a far-off cluster of vapor-blue peaks, where the Raft River Mountains girded the northern view.

In recording his impressions of the lake, Captain Stansbury truly defines the sensations produced by this view: "Although so near a body of the saltest water," he felt none of that "invigorating freshness which is always experienced in the vicinity of the ocean." "The bleak and barren shores," he goes on to say, " without a single tree to relieve the eye, presented a scene so different from what I had pictured in my mind of this far-famed spot, that my disappointment was extreme."

As the afternoon advanced the air grew sultry. The great briny surface

West Shore of Antelope Island, Great Salt Lake—reached via the Union Pacific System.

before us began to gleam with intolerable brilliance, outstretching like a vast mirror of polished steel, with the sun's path across it, like that same steel at a molten heat. Not a breeze moving, we lifted the main sail for shade, and wearily waited our messmate's coming. Soon the western horizon melted away in a golden haze; islands and promontories floated in air; the distant mountain chains parted asunder, to become groups of peaked islands, or stretch across the sky like the arches of wondrous bridges. So unreal it became at last, so like a phantasmagoria, that substance and shadow were undistinguishable. In plainer words, all the strange illusions attending a mirage on the inland sea were witnessed to perfection that summer day.

It was just as the sun had dipped, that the prow of our yacht grated on the sands of Fremont Island. A couple of cabins stood on the shore, not a hundred yards away from our landing, and long ere we touched we had noticed a cloud of dust descending from the hill-tops toward them. This the glass made out to be caused by a single horseman, spurring along at a breakneck speed. From the shore we were greeted with a loud ahoy! to which we responded with a hearty cheer. Two noble deer-hounds and a noisy Scotch terrier came leaping to meet us; a solitary life at the lonely place had made them more gentle than fierce.

We found the island to have six inhabitants. The herdsman we had seen, the owner of the cabins, his wife, their two children, and a household servant. Cultivated plots surrounded the cabin, while a flock of sheep grazed on a neighboring hill-side. The water of the place is supplied by a flowing well, though this was obtained until recently from a natural spring near by.

Mutual greetings exchanged, we were naturally anxious to view the more important sights of the place. One of these is the spring just mentioned, and a remarkable pebble beach. The latter is a mile or more up shore, and is known by the name of Mosaic. Its bright, polished pebbles are of various colors, with a deep golden yellow conspicuous. Some are of a purple black, and others of a marble whiteness. Beside this beach there is a little alcove, where the pebbles are equally well polished, some of a pale, slaty gray, intermingled with others of a green and deep red hue.

While going along the trail, our captain told of a pitiable sight he had witnessed on a former visit. This had been about ten years before, when the lake was unusually high. With a single companion, he had crossed over to the island, and both men were engaged in searching for the spring, when a loud and continuous bleating directed their steps to the place. Arriving at the edge of an overhanging cliff, this sorry sight met their gaze. There on the beach stood, perhaps, a hundred sheep, huddled together, and looking appealingly at the spot where the spring had formerly been. In the agony of thirst they pawed furiously the shingle, fresh victims continually adding to the number of dead already lying by the shore. With throats parched and burning, the two men

Village on the Lake Shore, Great Salt Lake—reached via the Union Pacific Syst.m.

could well sympathize with the tortured animals. Seeing that their own quest for water was fruitless, they hurried away to their boat, and sped to the nearest water they knew, that of a spring near Promontory.*

With the words of this story fresh in our ears, we arrived at the spring, from whence we crossed over to the alcove on the opposite shore. Shadows of twilight hung over the place. Tints of ravishing beauty were on sky and water. Primrose-yellow filled the lower heavens, changing imperceptibly into vaguest green, with violet at the zenith. Dim along the horizon, chains of mountains formed bands of pearly rose, rose gray, and ashes of rose. In the lake deep amber took the place of the primrose, and wherever a breeze ruffled slightly its otherwise quiet surface, was reflected the violet hue, edged with the paly green.

Well pleased with the events of our third day out, we returned to the cabins. Our host read aloud some passages from Frémont's book, those narrating his visit to the Disappointment Island, as he called it, in company with Kit Carson, in 1843. "How little has it changed," said our host, "from its solitary condition at the time, save for these two little cabins, these plots of cultivated ground, and my one small flock of hardy sheep." †

Later on, all hands betook themselves again to the beach, there to enjoy the serenity of the summer night. Over the Wahsatch, above the gap formed by the Weber River, the moon had risen, shedding a flood of silvery radiance across the waters. The novelty of our situation, the loneliness of the time, gave a zest to the most commonplace story or anecdote, and, well! I was going to write how heartfelt sounded the music, but we all know that; the charm of out-door music is everywhere the same, one of the chief pleasures of being under the open sky, whether it be on spreading plain, under the shadow of granite hills, or, as with us, by the shore of a briny sea. Hail Columbia! Ye Banks and Braes o' Bonnie Doon. All in the Bay of Biscay, O! So we joined our voices

---

* Perhaps the above paragraph needs some explanation. The men had not visited the island before, and which was then uninhabited. The place bears an abundance of rich, sweet grass, and the sheep had been left there for winter pasturage. The unusual rise in the lake was certainly unlooked for. Besides this annual rise and fall, there has been of late years a permanent rise in its surface, enough to form the strait between Strong's Knob and the terminal rock of the Desert Range, and also to cover over several low-lying reefs and islands, that are now a source of considerable danger.

† In a life passed so much in isolation, one becomes intimately acquainted with the habits of the lower creatures around them. There are but few creatures native to the island, but with these few our host had become thoroughly in sympathy. A large species of lizard is quite numerous, and one of these became so tame as to be a daily playmate with the children. Several old ravens make the island summit their home. Their ominous croak may be heard at almost any time in vicinity of the flock. Forever they are on the lookout for some stray lamb or sheep that may have fallen among the cliffs. For that reason they have been condemned to death, but execution of the sentence is continually deferred.

G

On the Beach at Garfield, Great Salt Lake—on the Union Pacific System

RAND McNALLY CO

(18)

in song after song, national, gay, or pathetic, as the moment willed, and all the while the flood of moonlight outlined in umber the mast, the hull, the rigging, of our trusty yacht, and danced with the waves among the branches of a stranded old cedar, as the summer night wore away.

With the next few paragraphs is described the last twenty-four hours of our stay on the eastern shores. They were among the most fruitful of our entire circuit. The scenery on the west side of Antelope astonished us; we did not expect to see anything like it. The day, too, was in our favor, showing the peculiar atmospheric effects in a wonderful degree. Six years before, I had ridden along part of the same piece of shore, but in the month of August. Then the rocks and bushes were covered thick with a veil of cobwebs, the big, fat spiders making the beach a place to be avoided. To appreciate this scenery one should see it from a boat's deck, and in the months of early summer or autumn. One thing we would liked to have seen that day was the flash of a rival sail. From end to end of the island not a sign of human life had met our sight. An old cabin (once inhabited by salt gatherers) tumbling to pieces, its open door staring blankly at us, rather augmented than lessened the solitude of the place. With neither sail on the water, nor life on the land, we could easily have thought ourselves the first to cruise along its deserted shores.

Again upon the waters, our interest centered in watching the shifting forms of mountains and islands. At our back (our course was now southeast) a rounded mass of rock appeared to float on the water. This our guide pronounced as Strong's Knob, once a headland, now an island. Beyond this point and the end of Fremont, the eye traveled over an immeasurable stretch of water toward a range of mountains, spectral with extreme distance; the water was the northwest portion of the lake, and the mountains the barrier line in that direction of the ancient Bonneville. *

Noon found us on the coast of Antelope, becalmed in White Rock Bay. The hurrying rattle of the waves along the boat's side had changed to a lazy swash, finally ending in silence. Somnolence brooded over land and main; the motionless water lay unsullied; not even a troublesome gnat was aboard from the shore. Here was a chance for unparalleled bathing. Soon four mariners were sporting like Tritons in liquid green, whilst seated on deck, two timid ones, Satyr-like, looked wistfully on. †

* The outlet to this vast ancient body of water has been shown, by Professor Gilbert, to have been at a place now called Red Rock Pass, a deep defile cut through the mountains referred to. The lines formed by the old water-levels along the mountain sides affect the character of every scene. But few sketches were made on our cruise in which their strange individuality did not occur.

† Bathing in the lake is one of the most novel of sensations. The dense water has a tendency to float the limbs to the surface, so that one can sustain themselves in a recumbent position for an indefinite length of time, that is, when the water is anywise calm. It is hard work to make headway in swimming against even the smallest waves.

" There hung Venus, our beneficent Star," Great Salt Lake—reached via the Union Pacific System.

Davis Strait and Strong's Knob, Great Salt Lake—reached via the Union Pacific System.

From the upper reach, where we lay becalmed, the rock which has named the bay, appeared as if encrusted with glittering salt, but it is merely the whiteness of the rock itself. Its position in the center of the bay, together with the dark tones of the surrounding hills, makes it a very conspicuous object.

At a later hour, as we drifted near, with a few cat's-paws of wind, we noticed the suspicious actions of several gulls. Wheeling overhead, they appeared in deep distress. "See!" said one of our crew, "the gulls are nesting on yonder rock, and the herons are keeping sentinel." A glance revealed, as he said, the tall, blue-coated herons, and a moment later a whole troop of gulls dropped from the rock and came screaming toward us. The noise was deafening, as valiantly they dashed round our mast-head. In this they offered a striking contrast to the cowardly herons. With slow beat of wing the latter had flown shoreward, and then mounted far into the bright blue sky. When we grappled the rock, the rage of the gulls was furious; we could hardly keep them from off our faces. At last, finding assaults in vain, they suddenly deserted their home in a body, settled on the water near by, where, as from a fallen white cloud, sounded their continuous screaming and calling.

The afternoon was well advanced when we sailed down past a monster cliff known as the Elephant's Head. It forms the terminal point to the Monument Ridge, as the highest elevation of the island is called. Hanging over the pale green water, huge coils of a shining, whitish rock, twisted in among its contorted, gray strata, this iron-gray cliff is pictorially superb. After that came bay after bay, with ragged points, with needle spires, stacks, cubes, mounds, old molars of rock, fantastic forms innumerable. Close we ran our boat along this shore, beneath hills covered with parched, russet foliage, beneath mountains of fire-burnt rock, from which the stentorian voice of our mate awoke a series of witch-like echoes.

While the scenery to landward had kept our attention, there was appearing in the west an effect of light and color to be seen nowhere else on the American Continent. The water was green, yet such an indescribable green, beneath that blazing sun, and playing all over its surface were flame-like wavelets of pale blue. Distant mountains were violet and rose, the furthest eaten away with the white burning light of mirage. At sunset we witnessed one of those peerless displays of color for which the sea is famous. Called forth by the heat of the day, a pile of cloud had gathered along the southwestern horizon, and were moved between our course and the sun. Kind reader, this is not a plan, a device to give a grand scenic finale to our last day out. Long will we remember the resplendent spectacle! Girding the far horizon, the western mountains appeared like the outermost land of earth, resting on a sea of gold. When the sun touched the verge, it was as though we looked into a vast furnace of living flame. (Hats off, messmates! Hats off! Honor to the mighty orb, the sustainer of heat and light, in whose beams the joys, the sorrows of life, are transmitted

Desolate Shores, near Strong's Knob, Great Salt Lake—reached via the Union Pacific System.

(23)

from age to age, and in whose withdrawal would be the eternal apathy of
death.)

It was quite dusk when we reached the southern end of Antelope Island,
and a stronger breeze than we had enjoyed at any time of the day began to
speed us on. Should we take advantage of it and have a glorious night sail?
All were agreed to that. The prow of our boat, pointing to Garfield Beach, was
changed to Lakeside, a village on the eastern shore. Daylight, however,
found us once more becalmed several miles from our goal. With whiffs of wind
we crept nearer and nearer. From the pastures where cattle were browsing,
we heard the flute-notes of the meadow larks. Beautiful appeared the drooping
foliage in the orchards of the village, with the peeping gables above. To our
sharpened appetite the languid coils of smoke, issuing from the chimneys, told
a pleasant tale. We had just began to grow impatient of delay, to cast longing
glances shoreward, when a stiff breeze suddenly made taut our idle sails. Some-
one sprang to the tiller, the water commenced to feather gently from the bows,
and then form a curling line in our wake. It required but a short period of
such lively sailing to place us alongside of a rickety old pier, and bring our
initial cruise to a most agreeable end.

Taking all things into consideration, the lesser portion of our circuit of the
Great Salt Lake had certainly been a decided success. We had viewed the
many strange sights and places under the most favorable circumstances. We
looked forward anxiously for its second part, which was to take us out across
the main body of the lake, and to those islands and shores but rarely visited by
man. Gunnison Island, the farthest point we expected to touch, occupied a
place in my mind as a realization of perfect solitude; in summer the nesting-
place of countless birds, and in winter lying ghostly white, in its shroud of
snow, amid the blackness of unfreezing waters.

We arrived at the beach when there was promise of dirty weather. The
barometer had been steadily falling, and there was that sultry hush in the air
that tells of coming storm. We took no care, however, thinking it no cause for
delay; we expected to sail away from what might prove merely a local disturb-
ance, and to cast anchor where another wind-current prevailed. We respected,
though, even if we did not fear just then, the northwest gales. It was in defer-
ence to these we had planned the course of the present cruise. In working
northward along the base of Stansbury Island, we would be shielded somewhat
from meeting with adverse seas, and also escape beating against them in crossing from Gunnison to Promontory, over a part of the lake that is especially
subject to heavy blows.

Without dwelling upon the incidents of the opening hours, in which we
passed the mouth of Tuilla Valley, and reached the island (Stansbury), I shall
begin to relate from the morning of the second day. All signs of the storm had
disappeared, the sunrise bringing with it a mildly blowing wind from the south.

Edge of the Desert, from Crow's Nest, Great Salt Lake—reached via the Union Pacific System.

With mainsail and foresail set wing to wing (an oar converted into a spinnacher boom) we moved slowly along; so slowly indeed, that our mate swam ashore to examine a stranded boat, lying high and dry on the rocks. From the great holes broken in its side, he concluded it to have been cast there by some winter storm, a supposition borne out by its being just on the edge of the highest surf line.

Once away from the island, there was an overpowering sense of solitude in the waste of waters round. A golden-gray sunset closed in the peaceful day, followed by the earliest stars. Such a meal as we enjoyed out there, under the twilight sky! Was there an epicure in all the land brought such an appetite to his supper as we? While we glided along, gently, as if wafted through air, a great blue heron came from a lonely rock near by, to sail over our boat with outstretched pinions. When he had gone, a shout turned all eyes to the northward: "Gunnison Island, ahoy!" a purple speck no bigger than a lad's top peeping above the horizon rim.

The discovery just narrated was made at the beginning of a splendid sail. The wind had been momentarily growing less in our vicinity, though there was a *sparkler* coming down from the head of the lake—such a one as tossed up the white-caps in a hurry. Sometimes we doubted if the dark, tiny speck could be Gunnison Island or no, so small it appeared amid the area of waves. Once we lost sight of it altogether, yet it reappeared, the expiration of a few hours showing it to be the highest peak of the island.

I said at the beginning of a splendid sail: Can we ever forget those hours of joyful life between the evening and morning twilight? Held close to the wind, veering round to the west, we sped on at a rate that sent the water reeling in our wake with the swiftness of a mountain torrent. Our boat was all aqueous, and to hold the tiller was like keeping in check an impetuous steed. Had our cruise ended that night, still it would have been worth more than a year of every-day life. How like a dream it was to be out there on the face of that mysterious sea! How like a dream to be moving in the deep midnight toward the shadows of its unknown shores! Every sight and every sound had in it something of wonder or beauty. There hung Venus, our beneficent star. All of the islands had long disappeared, though the small lonely rock, the home of the heron, was visible again for a moment, as, fiery and big, the moon arose like a midnight sun from the waters. A glorious, never-to-be-forgotten night; all the world and its troubles seeming as far away as though we had voyaged to another planet across the waves of a nebulous sea!

> "Midnight's sun, all blood-red bright,
> Far-off isles o'er-bended;
> It was not day, it was not night,
> Between them 'twas suspended."

From the edge of Strong's Knob, where we landed next morning, can be seen a most characteristic view of the western shore. The sketch was made as

Pelican Bay, Gunnison Island, Great Salt Lake—reached via the Union Pacific System.

we skirted along the beach of a little bay, on the way to climb the highest eminence of the island. It is looking diagonally across the Davis Strait toward
the mouth of the American Desert. Desolation brooded over the original
scene, and yet there was mingled with its peculiarities a weird sort of witch-
like beauty, strange to behold. The fantastic rocks jutting out from the land
may be duplicated on many a sea-shore, but not the blended pallor and purity
of color which marked the place. Not the slightest humidity arose from the
water, only that wavy heat-haze that made the distance float in a dreamy
mirage.

From the top of the peak, a view, oppressive from its very immensity, greeted
the sight. Very little wind was moving, so in the shallows the lake lay quiet,
among the numerous sand-bars of the strait, more like green, translucent ice,
than water. From the cro-nest, erected by Stansbury, the outlook was wild.
Far, and away to the west, stretched the whiteness of the awful desert. Vast-
ness and strangeness were the leading features. Yet rather than be slaves to
these, we sought refuge in examining the nearer shores of the Knob. One of
its projecting arms seemed designed by nature to show the principles of the
picturesque. Its irregular outline included five miniature bays, each with its
overhanging rocks, and its beach of pure, white sand. These bays are so situ-
ated as to give shelter from the wind, blow from what quarter it may.

In a limited area, its entire shore-line can not exceed three miles. Gunnison
Island, our Ultima Thule, exhibits as many diversified forms as can be found on
a rough sea-coast. It has beetling cliffs, sandy beaches, walls and pyramids of
rock, and stacks pinnacled and grottoed, and inhabited by crowds of screaming
sea-fowl. In some respects it may be likened to an outlying fragment of "sea-
beat Hebrides;" but on a summer day, with the fervid heat pouring down on the
lava rocks, with its lizards darting across the burning sands, the green and blue
water, lying glassy calm, and on the horizon gleams of snow-crested peaks, it
more closely resembles some lonely rock of the Azores. Well could we ask,
Where could we find another such lake, with another such island, where, in the
noon of a summer day, we might fancy ourselves by the shore of some southern
sea, and yet be standing on a spot that is howled across by the fiercest of winter
storms?

No sooner had we leaped on its shore, than our first impulse was to cross
a neck of land over which a snow-white gull had risen with clamour. Such a
shout as we gave, and such an answering scream from the throats of myriad birds!
Not in our circumnavigation of the lake had we looked upon another scene
half as picturesque as that, nor one whose sombre features were enlivened with
such a multitude of noisy life. Every hour of our stay at this island was filled
with the echoes of a ceaseless din. When in our ramblings from bay to bay
we happened to pass through the colonies, the fury of this tumult arose to its
greatest height.

Cliffs of Gunnison Island, Great Salt Lake—reached via the Union Pacific System.

For an hour we thought of nothing but watching their ways. Besides the hundreds of thousands of clamorous gulls, there was rank behind rank of the more stolid pelicans. It is a pity to spoil the pleasing impression made by a first sight of these birds, by a subsequent closer acquaintance. Their effect in the sea-scape is splendid. Along the marge of the shore they stand wing to wing, motionless as well-drilled soldiers. No bird could be more dignified in slow-measured flight; while afloat on the water they are graceful as swans.

The sketch for the cliffs at Promontory was made when the lake was placid, our yacht lying in the shadow of the cliffs, waiting for a favoring breeze. One of the peculiarities of the lake is the suddenness with which it can become calm after running high. That very morning we had a highly exciting time in crossing to the Point from Gunnison Island. As that run gives a good idea of what it is, at times, to sail on the inland sea, I write it in full.

At an early hour we quitted the island. Land and water were vaguely defined in a struggle between moonlight and dawn. The mainsail of our yacht was double-reefed, for we had some misgivings of the weather outside; the wind had been dead to the north, and blowing hard since dark. On one side of the cliffs the water was calm, but whenever we awoke in the night we could hear the crash of the waves in the opposite bay, and the cry of the troubled gulls, as they broke on the beach, where their young were nested.

Half a mile from the shore and we began to catch the breeze; not very boisterous at first, but enough to make the island drop rapidly astern, so that in less than an hour it looked farther away than Strong's Knob to the south, its outline exceedingly grand.

By that time, however, there was very little chance for admiring the scene, winds and waves had increased, until the latter would have tossed a good-sized ship. The point we wished to make lay somewhat south of east, so our course lay nearly along the trough of the sea; but in order to quarter the waves, we had to direct our course more northerly, to a point some miles up shore. With the waves so high, with the winds increasing, anxious faces might have been seen on board our boat; not but that we expected to weather it through, but when it taxed the strength of two hardy men to manage the tiller of such a tiny craft, affairs were getting decidedly critical. Perhaps those who were landsmen overestimated the danger, but still I believe that every man on board devoutly wished himself on shore; not in any craven way; perish the thought! not to have evaded the danger then and there, and thus have missed its lesson, but wishing, rather, that we had fought it successfully through. All men, save born cowards, must know of the thrill, the secret sense of exultation, engendered by looking a danger full in the face; to fully realize its presence, yet not turn aside. To those who pass their life in continual security must sometimes come a longing, the knowledge of a sense not satisfied. In the present case it might be argued there was no way of escape; true, but under similar circum-

At Rest, Promontory Point, Great Salt Lake—reached via the Union Pacific System.

stances no one need to expect to make a circuit of the Great Salt Lake without incurring the same kind of risks.

By sunrise the blow had come to its hardest.   The waves had a spiteful, vicious look, with the foam torn fiercely from off their crests. We had a trying moment as we dropped the mainsail, a towering wave striking the boat a blow that surrounded it for the moment in hissing foam; the next we were high on a crest, the foresail holding us steadily enough to the wind.

That was the turning point; the waves grew no higher; we fancied they were growing less. The sight was magnificent as the sun, lifting above a low bank of clouds, streamed on the turbulent sea. Struck by the level rays of light, how old the mountains appeared ; centuries of age seemed suddenly heaped on their heads. Toward the sun how beautiful it was ! The high waves pierced through by the light, so that they came forward like craggy walls of emerald below, and topaz above. It realized Byron's

> "The yellow beam he throws
> Gilds the green wave, that trembles as it glows."

But those lines were not meant for such a wild, tumultuous onsweeping of water such as we looked upon.

In another hour we had reached comparative calm. Sheltered by the tall Promontory hills, the lake only acknowledged the past blow by running in short, jerky swells, the most trying to landsmen of all motions of water.

On the afternoon of that same day we entered the bay at Fremont Island. We skimmed across nearly to its south horn, and then made landing on a sharp tack. Gilert, one of the hounds, manifested the greatest pleasure at our arrival, and a right cordial reception we again received from our island friends. The breeze that brought us gallantly in was but a temporary one; since the blow, a few such had been moving here and there on the lake, making dark ripple patches, like the shadows of passing clouds. While coming through the strait between the island and Promontory we made our stop at the latter. The scene was so very striking that we lay to, for the purpose of sketching. A bluff of light-colored sandstone jutted out boldly over the water, with lower projections of slate. The mountains across the lake showed beautifully, especially looking toward Stansbury Island, whose two high domes stood darkly shadowed against the sharp, dim snow-peaks of Tuilla Range. Over their summits was a towering cumulus, lovely in form and color. Seen near by, it was probably of a dazzling whiteness on its illuminated parts, with a suggestion of thunder in the lurid shadows, but at the distance we viewed, it showed on the sky in the most exquisite aerial tones.

With the foregoing our descriptions are ended; but it may not be out of place to give here a few remarks on the pleasures and dangers attending a cruise on the inland sea. It bears the unenviable reputation of being a most danger-ous sheet of water, and although there is no doubt but that the reputation is

Mirage Effect, No. 1, Great Salt Lake.

well merited, there are no reasons why it should not also be a source of much pleasure.   For carelessness, for bravado, there is certainly no room when traversing its saline waters.   The craft employed should be a stout one, fit to meet the strain of heavy seas, for in a sail of any length one is most likely to be met with.   It is almost incredible to those whose experience has been confined to fresh-water lakes to realize the force with which the heavy waves can strike, and yet in spite of its density, the water has a peculiar aptitude for transmitting motion; in a short time the waves rise to a trying height, though, as stated before, they fall as quickly on the cessation of a blow.

With a strong northwester, or 'easter, it is better not to venture forth at all. Our experience in running from the Gunnison to Promontory contained all the elements of danger the average boatman cares to face, and certainly as much as the average landsman cares to share.   The superiority of a catamaran over the ordinary boat was then fully demonstrated.   Although so light, our yacht was quite equal to the strain imposed upon her.   This strain was all the greater through the shallowness of the water.   The wave-crests were terribly close together; no such valleys between them as in deep, open water.   The suddenness with which we rose first on a crest, then sank in a vale, was one of the unpleasant features.

Another thing to be avoided is an involuntary immersion in the lake.   A fall overboard in rough weather simply means death.   Nor is this unlikely to happen when we consider the jerkiness of a little craft among such waves.   It is not a question of endurance in swimming; a very few mouthfuls of the choking fluid puts an end to all that.   Such an accident occurred to one of an exploring party, but in really moderate weather.   Even then the poor fellow that met with the mishap was unfit for duty for the next forty-eight hours.

In making a cruise to the islands occupying the northwest part of the lake, care must be taken to carry a plentiful supply of water.   Too much forethought in this respect is better than the slightest negligence, for not a drop of water trickles forth on either island, or along a hundred miles of coast.   Shipwreck there would be attended by the ugliest possibilities.

But these are the very darkest sides of certain dangers that may be encountered, and need deter no one from enjoying a sail on this mountain-locked sea.   Of the pleasures attendant upon such a sail, I have endeavored to give a true statement in the preceding pages.   These, it has been shown, are of no mean order.   A vast body of water on which one may float day after day, without twice looking on the same shores, certainly offers great attraction in the way of boating.   When, added to this, we consider the splendor of the effects, the attraction must be conceded to be noteworthy in many ways. Other trips were made by our party later than those described, but as they were, for the most part, over portions of our previous cruise, they will be omitted.   One was in the month of September, between two autumn storms.   The lake was

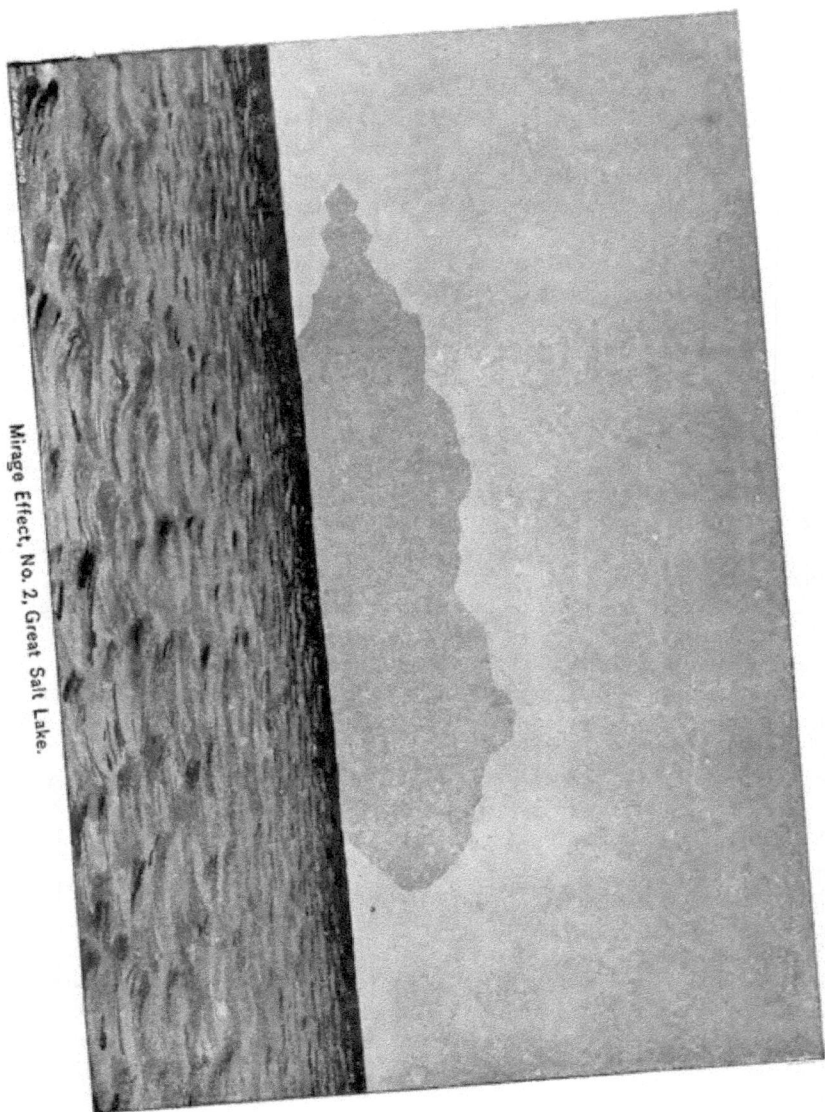

Mirage Effect, No. 2, Great Salt Lake.

quiet, the winds were soft. Dim, through ambient haze, the surrounding mountains loomed up; along their summits, newly-fallen snow; upon their feet,
brilliant dashes of color, where the fingers of the frost had touched.

In the accompanying diagrams I have placed together four notes of mirage
effect: three from the water, and one from the land. Figure one (1) is a bit of
the western shore detached by mirage and apparently floating in air; land and
reflection being indistinguishable, and the horizon melted away. In figure two
(2) there is the same effect of land and reflection, but there, instead of appearing to float in air, it produces the semblance of some strange barge moving
along the horizon. This horizon, of course, is a false one, and is caused by a
breeze moving on the nearer water, while that beyond is calm, and lost in the
sky.

In color there is a witchery about the mirage far beyond the reach of the
artist's palette. Thus in figure two (2) the sky was golden gray, absolutely
dazzling with light, while the island and its reflection was a fiery, yet perfect
blue. In figure three (3) again an effect of islands floating in air; the color
was altogether exquisite. Gold-gray sky, gold-white clouds, with distant water
same tint as the sky, which it appeared to be. Nearer, the water a pale, almost
invisible green, crossed not by waves, but with faint blurs of opalescent blue,
caused by the faintest, gentlest touch of winds.

There is another beautiful effect, also entirely local. It is seen during the
calm summer twilight, when the pale, fairy-like tints are breathed upon slightly
by opposite currents of wind. As they interplay in bands, in points, in shifting
isles of amber, azure, and rose, the whole lake surface shimmers and gleams,
like a silken robe, studded with countless pearls.

A world-wide traveler, speaking of the lake as seen from Garfield Beach,
has said: "Few persons, I think, realize how wonderfully, strangely beautiful
is this inland sea;" and another, "Where have I not seen sunsets, by land and
sea, in Asia, Africa, Europe, and America, and where can I say I have seen
more wondrous coloring, more electrifying effects, than in the Great Salt Lake
of Utah!" All of this is true; but much more could they have said had they
cruised with us from shore to shore, from north to south, from east to west,
and viewed it under the magic changes of sunshine, storm, and calm, as we did;
had seen it rage beneath the thunderstorms of June, and reflect the gorgeous-
ness of color painted on the clouds of autumn; had watched the weird effects
of the summer mirage; had looked upon the strangeness of the desert places
"where no man comes" that are washed by the waves of that briny sea!

                                        ALFRED LAMBOURNE.

Mirage Effect, No. 3, Great Salt Lake.

(37)

STANDARD PUBLICATIONS

PASSENGER AND TICKET DEPARTMENT OF THE UNION PACIFIC SYSTEM.

The Passenger and Ticket Department of the Union Pacific System will take pleasure in forwarding to any address, free of charge, any of the following publications, provided that with the application is enclosed the amount of postage specified below for each publication. All of these books and pamphlets are fresh from the press, many of them handsomely illustrated, and accurate as regards the region of country described. They will be found entertaining and instructive, and invaluable as guides to and authority on the fertile tracts and landscape wonders of the great empire of the West. There is information for the tourist, pleasure and health seeker, the investor, the settler, the sportsman, the artist, and the invalid.

A GLIMPSE OF GREAT SALT LAKE. Send 4 cents for postage.

This is a charming description of a yachting cruise on the mysterious inland sea, beautifully illustrated with original sketches by the well-known artist, Mr. Alfred Lambourne, of Salt Lake City. The startling phenomena of sea and cloud and light and color are finely portrayed. This book touches a new region, a voyage on Great Salt Lake never before having been described and pictured.

BILLIARD AND POOL RULES. Send 4 cents for postage.

This pamphlet contains all the existing rules governing the games of Billiards and Pool, and may be relied upon as exhaustive and accurate.

COMPREHENSIVE PAMPHLETS. Send 6 cents postage for each pamphlet.

A set of pamphlets on Colorado, Wyoming, Montana, Utah, Idaho, Oregon, Kansas, Texas, and Washington. These books treat of the resources, climate, acreage, minerals, grasses, soil, and products of these various empires on an extended scale, entering very fully upon an exhaustive treatise of the capabilities and promise of the places described. They have been very carefully compiled, and the information collated from official reports, actual settlers, and residents of the different States and Territories.

CROFUTT'S OVERLAND GUIDE, No. 1. Send 50 cents.

This book has just been issued. It graphically describes every point, giving its history, population, business resources, etc., etc., on the line of the Union Pacific System, between the Missouri River and the Pacific Coast, and the tourist should not start West without a copy in his possession. It furnishes in one volume a complete guide to the country traversed by the Union Pacific System, and can not fail to be of great assistance to the tourist in selecting his route, and obtaining complete information about the points to be visited.

FROM SUMMERLAND TO THE AMERICAN ALPS. Send 4 cents for postage.

This is a short description of that magnificent country traversed by the "Texas Panhandle Route," recently made a part of the Union Pacific System. It will be found a handy volume for Southern tourists who intend visiting the North during the summer.

(Continued on page 40.)

(35)

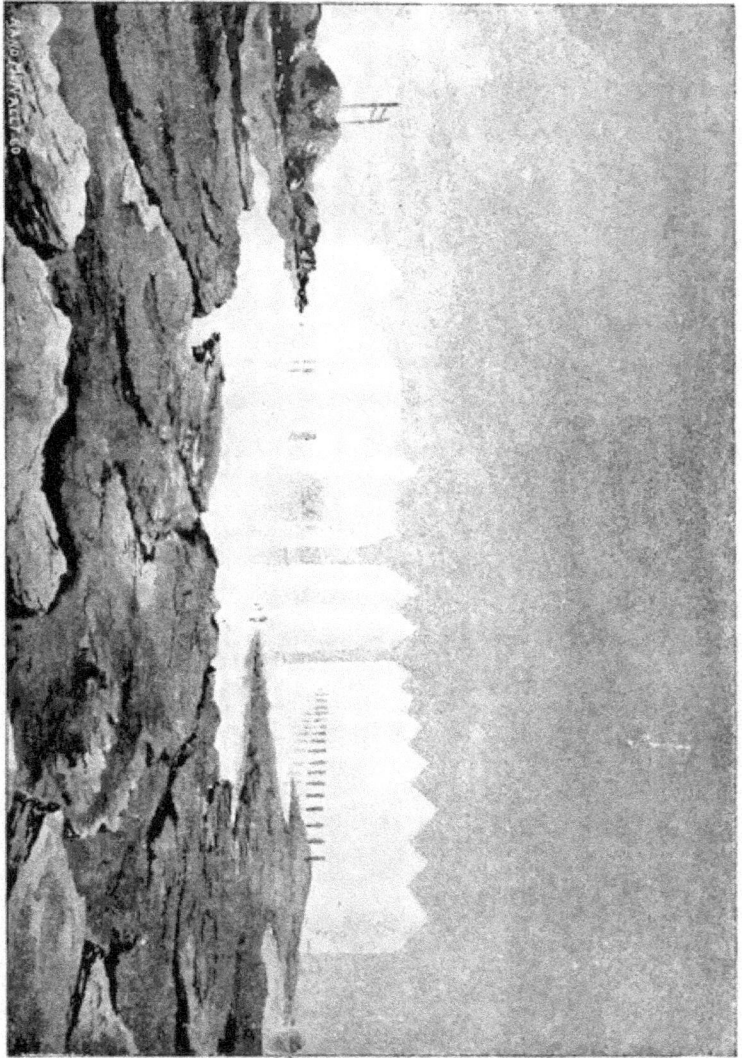

Mirage Effect, No. 4, Great Salt Lake.

GENERAL FOLDER. No postage required.

A carefully revised General Folder is issued regularly every month. This publication gives condensed through time tables; through car service; a first-class map of the United States, west of Chicago and St. Louis; important baggage and ticket regulations of the Union Pacific System, thus making a valuable compendium for the traveler and for ticket agent in selling through tickets over the Union Pacific.

GUN CLUB RULES AND REVISED GAME LAWS. Send 2 cents for postage.

This valuable publication is a digest of the laws relating to game in all the Western States and Territories. It also contains the various gun-club rules, together with a guide to all Western localities where game of whatsoever description may be found. Every sportsman should have one.

MAP OF THE UNITED STATES. Send 25 cents for postage.

A large wall map of the United States, complete in every particular, and compiled from the latest surveys; just published; size 46 x 66 inches; railways, counties, roads, etc., etc.

OUTDOOR SPORTS AND PASTIMES. Send 2 cents for postage.

A carefully compiled pamphlet of some thirty pages, giving the complete rules for Lawn Tennis, Base Ball, Croquet, Racquet, Cricket, Quoits, La Crosse, Polo, Curling, Foot Ball, etc., etc. There are also diagrams of a Lawn Tennis Court and Base Ball diamond. This pamphlet will be found especially valuable to lovers of these games.

PATHFINDER. No postage required.

A pamphlet of some sixty pages devoted to local time cards; containing a complete list of stations with the altitude of each; also connections with western stage lines and ocean steamships; through car service; baggage and Pullman Sleeping Car rates and the principal ticket regulations, which will prove of great value as a ready reference for ticket agents to give passengers information about the local branches of the Union Pacific System.

SIGHTS AND SCENES. Send 2 cents postage for each pamphlet.

There are six pamphlets in this set, illustrated, and are descriptive of tours to particular points. The set comprises "Sights and Scenes in Colorado;" Utah; Idaho and Montana; California; Oregon and Washington, and Alaska. Each pamphlet deals minutely with every resort of pleasure or health within its assigned limit, and will be found bright and interesting reading for tourists.

STREAM, SOUND, AND SEA. Send 2 cents for postage.

A neat, illustrated pamphlet, descriptive of a trip from the Dalles of the Columbia to Portland, Ore., Astoria, Clatsop Beach; through the Strait of Juan de Fuca and the waters of the Puget Sound, and up the coast to Alaska. A handsome pamphlet containing valuable information for the tourist.

THEATRICAL DIARY. Send 10 cents for postage.

This is a Theatrical Diary for 1892-93, bound in Turkey Morocco, gilt tops, and contains a list of theatres and opera houses reached by the Union Pacific System, seating capacity, size of stage, terms, newspapers in each town, etc., etc. This Diary is intended only for the theatrical profession.

"THE OLDEST INHABITANT." Send 10 cents for postage.

This is a buffalo head in Sepia, a very artistic study from life. It is characterized by strong drawing and wonderful fidelity. A very handsome acquisition for parlor or library.

VEST POCKET MEMORANDUM BOOK. Send 2 cents for postage.

A handy, neatly gotten-up little memorandum book, very useful for the farmer, business man, traveler, and tourist.

WESTERN RESORT BOOK. Send 6 cents for postage.

This is a finely illustrated book, describing the vast Union Pacific System. Every health resort, mountain retreat, watering place, hunter's paradise, etc., etc., is depicted. This book gives a full and complete detail of all tours over the line, starting from Sioux City, Council Bluffs, Omaha, St. Joseph, Leavenworth, or Kansas City, and contains a complete itinerary of the journey from either of these points to the Pacific Coast.

WONDERFUL STORY. Send 2 cents for postage.

The romance of railway building. The wonderful story of the early surveys and the building of the Union Pacific. A paper by General G. M. Dodge, read before the Society of the Army of the Tennessee, September, 1888. General Sherman pronounced this document fascinatingly interesting and of great historical value, and vouched for its accuracy.

(40)